HOW TO RAISE AN EVERYDAY HERO: QUOTES FOR BEDTIME AND BEYOND

KEVIN BINGHAM

HOW TO RAISE AN EVERYDAY HERO:

QUOTES FOR BEDTIME AND BEYOND

Kevin Bingham

With special thanks to Nikki Bingham for her ideas, inspiration, and review.

I dedicate this book to my children, Alex and Nikki. Without your willingness to listen to daddy's favorite quotes, power point presentations, and motivational books, this book would not have been possible. I know you've heard the Bingham motto 10,000 times, but here it is for the 10,001st time: "Whatever you put your mind to, you can do it!" May it be forever in your heart and always on your mind.

I love you both.

This book is a work of fiction.

How to Raise an Everyday Hero: Quotes for Bedtime and Beyond
ISBN-13: 978-1505877816
ISBN-10: 1505877814

Printed in the United States of America
First Printing, 2015

Contents

Inspiration behind the Book

Kids love repeating things. A single phrase, jingle, or sound bite can become more than just something they say, it can become something they value. We want our kids to repeat and value more than what they see on TV or hear on the radio. Quotes are the perfect way to deliver a bite-sized moral message. Reading and repeating quotes reinforces life's important messages, even at an early age. The quotes help capture magical moments, illustrate virtues, inspire bigger dreams, and pass on the wisdom from previous generations.

Think about the last quote that really struck a chord in your heart. Did you wish there was a way to capture that moment or special feeling? Did you imagine sharing that moment with your family? When we raise everyday heroes, we cannot afford to let life's valuable lessons pass us by without taking a moment to share them with our children. *How to Raise an Everyday Hero* will teach you how to draw inspiration from normal, real life scenarios and use quotes, stories, discussion, and activities to reinforce those positive and powerful life messages.

I witnessed the power of quotes with my own daughter. Back in 2009, during a ride back from a family trip, my daughter Nikki created her own list of quotes. They included:

"Whatever you put your mind to you can do it."
"You do not have to be popular to make friends."
"Your life is yours, not others."
"Be you."

"Be successful in your life."
"Climb to the mountain top."
"Think before you act."
"Make your own decisions."
"Be positive in front of others."

It is an impressive list for an eight-year-old. After absorbing the words of motivational speakers, athletes, inventors, presidents, and authors we had read together, she created her own. Sharing positive quotes with my little girl shaped her character and stuck with her over the years—far beyond bedtime.

This book is a legacy for my children. It is a way to commemorate the quotes that brought us together and helped them grow to be my everyday heroes. Someday, I hope they can share this book with their own children.

When you put your children to bed tonight, follow the five steps described in this book and start shaping your own everyday heroes.

The Five Steps

Every parent wants to raise an everyday hero, so here are the Five Steps that will give you a repeatable method for sharing and reinforcing the right messages with your children.

The Five Steps

1. Read a quote together, and encourage your child to read it aloud.
2. Ask your child if they understand the quote.
3. Share what the quote means to you.
4. Ask your child to share an example of what the quote means to them.
5. Challenge your child to put the quote into practice.

In *How to Raise an Everyday Hero*, each chapter focuses on a different virtue and a different character. We will follow the adventures of several everyday heroes, like Unipeg, the half Pegasus, half Unicorn.

Each chapter has five sections: a main quote, a virtue introduction, a story, discussion questions, and games and activities. We also have other special quotes throughout the chapter to reinforce the virtue. These quotes should inspire you and your child not only the first time you read them, but also as you revisit the values and challenges of raising an everyday hero.

Raising an everyday hero is a commitment, and I hope that this book helps you build and maintain a life-long relationship with your children. Let's walk through an example of the Five Steps and how you should approach each chapter.

A Five Step Example

Step 1: Read a quote together—encourage your child to read it aloud.

In each chapter, you will find a full-page quote that sets the tone for the chapter. For example:

"To begin with the end in mind means to start with a clear understanding of your destination."

- Seven Habits of Highly Effective People

Stephen Covey

"Hi, I'm Prog, the pink frog. You will read about my courage later, but I'm here to remind you that it's OK to read the first chapter quote together. Sometimes I don't understand the quotes the first time, so my parents and I repeat it a few times so that the meaning really sinks in."

Step 2: Ask your child if they understand the quote.

The second part of each chapter includes a short description of the virtue and how it relates to being an everyday hero. Read the description to your child to introduce them to the virtue and how they might practice it. Then, read the quote that follows this description and ask your child questions like:

Whom do you think of when you read the quote?
When would you use this quote?
What does the quote mean to you?
Do you know why this quote relates to this virtue?

 "Hi I'm Spots, the chihuahua. Even though I am a leader now, I didn't always like being the first to answer a question. When I was in pre-school and kindergarden, my parents mostly just read the quotes to me. They only wanted me to understand what the quote meant. The main focus was having fun and spending quality time together at night, not answering the question right or wrong."

Step 3: Share an example of what the quote means to you.

Some of my favorite stories as a kid were the ones my parents shared from their own childhood. In a young child's eyes, parents have it all: they have the answers, the decision-making power, and the amazing life experiences. Don't gloss over the moments when you were less than perfect kids, or when you struggled with a similar challenge. It could be the long process of saving up enough money for a new toy, the challenge of obtaining your merit badges for Cub Scouts, the practice required to stay on the sports travel team, or the anxiety of competing in a gymnastic event. Your child can relate to these moments. They realize that you were like them, and they don't have to be perfect to end up a hero.

When selecting a personal experience, I like to use an example that will resonate with my children. For example, here is how Utty might explain the concept of beginning with the end in mind to my children:

"Alex and Nikki, let me give you an example. Remember when one of your daddy's good friends called up and invited your family to a wedding in Texas? Your family had two months until the big day. Did your dad get in his car in Connecticut and start driving two months from the call, hoping to make it to the church on time?

No, first he asked for the exact date of the wedding, the name and address of the church, and the time your family should arrive. After that he thought about transportation. Your dad couldn't just walk to Texas, and even driving would take him a long time, so he had to buy plane tickets. Next, he needed a place to stay. What about the clothes he needed to pack? How about a toothbrush and toothpaste? Most importantly, your mom and dad would decide which toys you could bring and the movies for the car or flight.

By beginning with the end in mind, your family would have a clear picture of how to make it to the wedding on time."

The story section of each chapter serves as a supplement to your personal story. These short stories focus on considering different actions, overcoming inner conflicts, and respecting yourself and others. Each character shows traits of an everyday hero to help your child understand what being a hero might look like.

Step 4: Ask your child to share an example of what the quote means to them.

Hearing your personal story or reading the short story from each chapter should encourage children to share their own example. Simply repeating the quote does not mean your child understands it. By explaining the quote in their own words or connecting it to their own personal experiences, your child shows you that they understand. Sometimes the quote can be tricky and difficult to understand. In these cases, use the discussion question portion for inspiration and help.

 "Hi, I'm Cupcake, the polar bear. When I was little, my parents shared their stories or examples first, but now I want to create and share my own! I still love story time, but sometimes my older sister pretends to be asleep because she thinks she's too old for stories. I never want to be too old for stories!"

Step 5: Challenge your child to put the quote into practice.

Words on a page won't hold a child's attention for long. Transforming quotes and virtues into something real or interactive snatches back their attention. Our kids need to practice the virtue—and have fun doing it. The activities help our kids engage with the quote in an interactive way and make the evening more enjoyable and fun.

 "Hi, I'm Sunny, the pug. I love staying up late, but I have to be responsible and get rest so that I'm not too tired in the morning. Sometimes Mom and Dad will play a game with me before bed. After each story, you will see some of our favorite games and then a longer activity.

My parents say I'm practicing the virtue, but I'm just having fun!"

The games and activities are broken into two categories:
1. Just for fun character activities require little or no effort.
    2. Stretch activities require a time investment.

The stretch activities give your child the opportunity to practice the virtue. The just for fun games may not always sound educational, but their subtle messages will stick. The just for fun activities are included for parents like myself who were often times crunched for time during the weeknights. Try to do the activity with your child and reference the quote before and after.

I hope you have as much fun using quotes with your everyday hero as I did!

Acknowledgements

Throughout my life, I have benefited from an overabundance of love and support. It is nearly impossible to thank everyone, but let me take the time to especially thank those who helped make this book possible.

To my wife Terri: thank you for being my best friend, sounding board, occasional dance partner, and wonderful mother. I see a little more of you in Alex and Nikki every day.

To Alex and Nikki: thank you for being my willing test subjects. Bedtime reading was the highlight of my days and will always be a cherished memory. We shared quotes, stories, laughs, and love, and we will continue to do so for years to come. Both of you will go far. I could not be a prouder father.

To my parents: thank you for providing me the foundation and inspiration to become who I am today. If I had a dollar for every time someone told me how lucky I was to have my parents, I would be on the Forbes list of World's Billionaires. However, the real worth of family is beyond measurable wealth. Mom and Dad, you are amazing. The values you instilled in Brian and I made us into the upstanding men we are today. Your example taught us to be humble, respectful, honest, hardworking, inquisitive, and caring.

To my "Brother Bing": you are the best. The time we spend together with our families now brings me back to the days of our youth when we had so much fun making wrestling movies, playing outside, conquering video games, and folding laundry. Luckily, my math has gotten better from the days when we both "folded more than half" of the laundry.

To my Airport Gulf hockey family and best friend, Scott Gilbert: thank you for the years of fun, support, and life-long friendships. Our unforgettable 89 game winning streak, Wednesday night wings, JK's lake house, and family outings (e.g., Red Rose Pizza, annual Salem Croft Inn dinner, etc.) solidified our friendship and created a lifetime of memories. I look forward to growing older together, running more Tough Mudders, and joining the Over 80 League for a reunion season.

I must thank my team of reviewers: Kathy & Russ Bingham, Brian & Bobbi Bingham, Chris Morelli, Dana Murphy, Greg Chrin, Anne Crapo, Jennifer Bailey, and Lisa Disselkamp for their thoughtful comments and review.

I would like to thank our illustrator, Kim Porazzo. She did a fantastic job of bringing Nikki's toys and the stories to life.

Last but not least, I would like to thank my editor, Rachel Disselkamp. Without our introduction, I am not sure this book would have been possible. Rachel's energy, critical eye, and commitment to making this book a reality kept me inspired throughout production. I will be forever grateful that we collaborated on this book. You are truly an everyday hero to me.

Stars of the Hero Journey

Before getting started, let's meet the real-life stars of *How to Raise an Everyday Hero*:

Each story focuses on a particular event in the fictional life of one of my daughter's favorite toys. You will meet Utty the Cow, Cupcake the Polar Bear, Spots the Chihuahua, Sunny the Pug, Prog the Pink Frog, and Unipeg the Half-Unicorn and Half-Pegasus. These everyday heroes do not have buildings named after them or monuments commemorating their heroic act, their towns do not have parades to celebrate their heroism, and they don't ever win an Olympic medal. These everyday heroes wear their hero badges on the inside; their reward is bettering themselves and others. I invite you to share their journeys and see how you too can practice everyday heroism.

Meet the Everyday Heroes

Utty   Cupcake   Sunny

Prog   Unipeg   Spots

After each story, our characters will suggest a few of their favorite "just for fun" games. These might be new games or they might be old, but either way, these games are just for having for fun!

courage

IS THE **most** IMPORTANT OF ALL **virtues** BECAUSE WITHOUT COURAGE, YOU CAN'T PRACTICE ANY OTHER VIRTUE consistently.

Maya Angelou, writer and poet

Courage

Everyday heroes are courageous. They have the strength to face danger and difficulty. Courage takes confidence, but you can still be afraid. Courageous people take risks even if they might be scary, hard, or unpopular. You do not have to lift a car off the train tracks or run into a burning building to be courageous. You can be brave by saying, "I'm sorry," when you have hurt someone, or admitting when you are wrong. You could stand up for a classmate or ask someone lonely to dance with you. Even riding a big roller coaster, getting a shot at the doctor's office, or zip lining takes courage.

Courage is like a muscle: the more you use it the stronger you become. It may require a sacrifice, like exercising when you might not want to, but if you do not practice, your courage muscle becomes weak over time. Even the best athletes still have to be brave enough to join a team, confident enough to compete, and daring enough to try even when it might hurt. If you are a real everyday hero you won't let fear or laziness get in your way. You will exercise your courage muscles every day!

" All of your ....
.... **dreams** can come true-
if we have the courage
to **pursue** them. "

-Walt Disney, Founder of Disney

Leaving "Comfort" Behind

Prog sat alone on the seesaw, again. Prog was a little pink frog who could not jump. Every day he watched his three best friends, Hop, Skip, and Jumpy, sneak out of the playground and leap over the reed wall into the great unknown. Oh, what adventures they had! Pouncing on mud-pies, leaping over logs, diving into deep water... leaving Prog behind to play alone.

"Come on, Prog! You can make it! Just try!" they called out. However, a high wall of cattails and reeds surrounded their lily pad village and separated Prog from his friends.

"I can't! Go on without me," Prog said sadly, plopping down on the seesaw. *I want to jump*, he thought, *but I just can't. I've already tried and am too scared to try again.*

Prog had never left the small lily pad village of Comfort. He was nearly 12 weeks old—almost a fully-grown frog—but he still could not jump over the reeds. Hop, Skip, and Jumpy had been jumping for weeks now. Prog could barely bounce.

Prog was convinced he had Wiggly Leg Syndrome, which made froggy legs wobble and shake. However, the doctor told his parents that he no real symptoms for Wiggly Leg Syndrome. With a little practice, he could jump like everyone else.

"It can't be true!" cried Prog when his parents gave him the test results.

"Prog is just a scaredy-tadpole," said Prog's older sister, Croakina, with an enormous grin. "*I* could jump when I was only 8 weeks old."

"Prog is taking his time," said Prog's mom whose long, slender legs helped her win many jumping championships in the past. "We know he's got it in him, he just needs to build up the courage to jump."

"Exactly. Prog will jump when he's ready," Prog's dad said with a big bullfrog smile.

Prog said nothing. He just looked down at his plate of stinky mealworms and flies.

After dinner, Prog swam sadly to his lily pad. The night sky was crystal clear and the air was cool. The only thing that cheered Prog up was seeing his favorite star twinkling above: The North Star. Just as he closed his big, bug-like eyes, Skip popped his head out from under the water.

"Prog!" Skip whispered loudly. "Prog, wake up! This is important!"

"What is it?" asked Prog, confused and tired.

"It's Hop and Jumpy. We split up after an alligator chased us beyond the reeds today. Now I can't find them!" said Skip. "Hurry, we need to help our friends before it is too late."

"Okay, but how can I help?" asked Prog as they swam across the village toward the reed wall.

"*You* are going to help me find Hop and Jumpy before the alligator does," replied Skip.

"You mean…I have to jump the wall?" cried Prog. "Skip, I've never left Comfort. You know I can't jump *by myself*."

"And you know I can't jump with you on my back, but our friends are in danger!" said Skip.

Prog tried to think of another solution, but jumping was the only way over the reed wall. But wait a minute. The playground…the seesaw! "Skip, we need to go to the playground," he said.

"Not now, Prog. Can't you see we are on an important mission?" said Skip.

"Yes, but I need your help. We will use the seesaw to catapult me over the reed wall!" said Prog. He was still a little scared about this, but his friends needed him.

When they arrived at the playground, it was very dark. They found the seesaw and Prog hopped on.

"Okay," he said nervously, "Now jump with all your might!"

Skip smiled and then soared into the black night sky, crashing down on the other seat with a mighty *THUMP*. The seesaw launched Prog like a rocket over the reeds.

With a *SPLAT* Prog landed in the water on the other side of the reeds. He could hear Skip hopping and laughing not far behind. He thought he heard whispers behind the beaver dam, and sure enough, it was Hop and Jumpy.

"Prog? You found us!" they cried. "Thank goodness. We are caught in some fishing line. Can you help untie us?" Prog quickly untangled the line and released Hop and Jumpy, then saw Skip rushing toward them.

"Dudes…I don't think we are alone," said Skip, nearly out of breath. As they peaked over the dam, they saw a pair of yellow, glowing eyes staring at them.

"The alligator!" cried Jumpy.

Prog had never seen an alligator, and he didn't want this to be the last one he ever saw. He looked around. "Let's get out of here," said Prog. "This way!" The others followed without knowing if Prog knew where to go.

Prog did not know where they were, but he knew the position of the North Star as well as he knew his webbed toes. He jumped from lily pad to tree stump to slippery rock, not even realizing that he was jumping.

He leapt over a fallen tree and reached the edge of the reed wall. The other three frogs quickly hopped over, leaving Prog alone once more. *I can make this*, he thought. He heard the alligator snapping through the fallen tree. It was now or never. Prog pumped his legs and jumped as high as he could. This time, he made it over the wall.

By the time the four frogs made it back, the entire village knew of Prog's bravery. Prog's parents rushed to him, making sure the alligator had not gobbled him up. After a big hug and a sigh of relief, Prog's parents told him how worried they were when they realized Prog had run off in the middle of the night. But they were also proud that he had the courage to help his friends. It would be a day Prog always remembered: the day he left his "Comfort" zone and found the courage to save his friends.

" Nobody ⋯⋯⋯⋯⋯⋯⋯⋯⋯

⋯⋯⋯ can **make** you feel
inferior without your
consent"

-Eleanor Roosevelt, humanitarian and first lady

⋯⋯⋯⋯⋯⋯⋯⋯⋯⋯⋯⋯

" You can't build ⋯⋯⋯⋯⋯

⋯⋯⋯ a **reputation** on what
you are going to do."

-Henry Ford, inventor

⋯⋯⋯⋯⋯⋯⋯⋯⋯⋯⋯⋯

Discussion Questions

Pick a few of these to discuss together tonight. You don't have to complete everything now. It's just a list of options, so pick a few of your favorites!

1. Why did Prog need courage to jump over the reeds? Do you think he blamed Wiggly Leg Syndrome?
2. Why did jumping over the reeds require courage for Prog?
3. Did Prog's friends have more courage because they jumped over the reeds first?
4. When do you think Prog was the most courageous in the story?
5. Does courage always involve risk? Why or why not?
6. What are your biggest fears? Does anyone in your family have any silly fears?
7. Is courage something you are born with or something you develop?
8. What sort of activities, events, or circumstances build courage?
9. What sort of jobs do you think require the most courage?
10. What would you do if you knew you would not make a mistake or fail?

10 Ways to Be More Courageous. Have you done any of these?

1. Do something by yourself for the first time (e.g., ride a bike, look under the bed, going down into a spooky basement, jump off the high dive, etc.)
2. Try a food you have never eaten.
3. Apologize for something you did wrong.
4. Sit next to the new kid on the bus.
5. Enroll in an after school activity.
6. Stand up for yourself.
7. Make a public speech at school or perform in a play.
8. Forgive someone who said or did something unkind to you.
9. Ask for help when you need it.
10. Calm yourself after a bad dream or look under the bed instead of asking Mom or Dad.

Prog's Just for Fun Activities

When Prog isn't jumping from the high dive or hopping away from alligators, he likes to play these games with his parents:

Spider Fang/Cobra Fang Tickles

Curl your pointer finger and middle finger into a scary fang, and tickle away. Scare tactics can vary from the slow motion approach, all the way to the staggered rapid-fire attack.

Waste Basket-ball

Crunch up some paper balls and shoot three pointers into your bedroom garbage can. You could use a box or bucket as a goal as well. If you can frog-hop while scoring a goal, you get double points!

Creepy Crawly Box

Do hairy spiders, slimy maggots, and gooey brains make your skin crawl? If so, many others share your fear of these scary items. What if there was a game to help you conquer these fears? Although this game may be best around Halloween, it can be adapted to many party themes.

Rules:

With the help of an adult, cut an arm-sized hole out of a large cardboard box (make sure there can be no peeking!) This will be your Stage of Bravery. Alternatively, you could use a blindfold for contestants.

When a new item in placed inside the box, a judge either labels it on the outside or tells the child the name of this Creepy Crawly item (e.g., brains). Then, have the child feel it (without looking) and try to guess what it really is. Do not pressure children if they do not want to play.

Here are a few suggested items to put in your box:

- Damp, Course Sponge – Brain
- Twisted pipe cleaners – Spider
- Pretzel Stick - Petrified Rat Tails
- Dried Apricots - Dried-up Tongues
- Cooked, Cold Spaghetti Noodles – Worms or veins
- Olives or Peeled Grapes in oil – Eyeballs
- Fake Fur – Werewolf tail
- Tines of a Plastic Fork - Vampire Teeth
- Soft Flour Tortilla or cooked lasagna noodles in oil - Skin
- Feed Corn – Teeth
- Corn Husk Silk – Hair

- Baby Dill Pickles with pistachio shells pushed into the tip - Witches fingers
- Over-cooked rice with raisins in cooking oil - Maggots and bugs
- Mango slices – Mummy tongues
- Pumpkin filling mixed with mini marshmallows –Brains or guts

Play as many times as you would like with as many participants. Excited squeals and screams are the prize for this game!

SOMETIMES YOU WILL give MORE THAN YOU RECEIVE AND sometimes YOU WILL GET BACK MORE THAN YOU GIVE. It's not about keeping score.

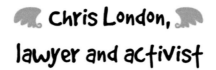 Chris London, lawyer and activist

Generosity

Everyday heroes are generous. Generous people are willing to give and do not expect a reward or gift in return. You do not have to be famous, rich, or powerful to be generous. You don't even need to give away all your money or your favorite toys. Everyday heroes can be generous by donating their time and special talents.

Many people want to be generous, but sometimes they just do not know how. Maybe you heard about a flood that destroyed a city in another state. Maybe you read about a local charity raising money for the development of a new baseball park. Maybe you heard about homeless dogs and cats in the local area without families, but you are unsure how to help.

Everyday heroes know that even small acts of generosity make a big impact. It is not about how *much* you give, it is about *what* you give and how willingly you give. Being generous means giving more than someone might need, ask for, or expect. Being generous means giving before getting and leaving people better off than when you first met them.

"A boy doesn't have to go to war to be a hero; he can say he **doesn't like pie** when he sees there isn't enough to go around."

-E.W. Howe, Newspaper and Magazine Editor

Every Coin Counts

" No one has ever become poor by giving."

—Anne Frank, Young Diarist

Unipeg picked out her outfit before sunrise that day: a blue sequin bathing suit, four white jelly sandals, and a sparkly silver bow for her horn. You have to look fancy for a pool party. Although Unipeg loved fashion, it was especially hard to find things that fit her. Unipeg was a very special animal. She was half unicorn and half Pegasus.

"Unipeg! Are you ready to take your bottles and cans to the recycling center?" called her mother, a brilliant white Unipeg with gentle eyes.

"Am I *ever!*" squealed Unipeg, rushing toward the mountain of cans and bottles.

Unipeg had waited weeks for this very summer day. She probably even dreamed about it. Unipeg had been collecting cans and bottles for a while now. She planned to turn them into the recycling center for five gold doubloons each.

"Don't forget that once you turn in all those cans, you get that toy you wanted," said her father, a tall and muscular horse with wings that spread out ten feet wide.

"I would *never* forget about that, Dad!" said Unipeg.

Unipeg was going to buy the Super-Duper-Splash-Splash-Blaster 3000. It would be the coolest toy at the pool party, guaranteed. Unipeg knew it would make her the most popular

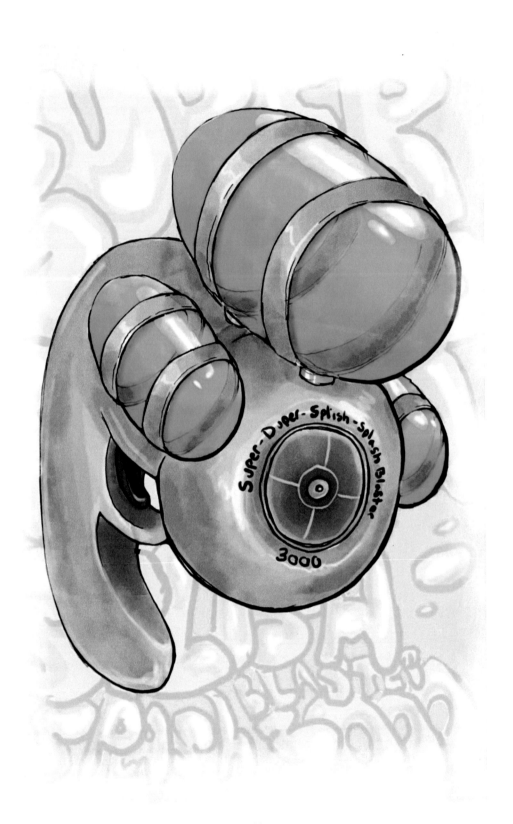

animal at the pool party. Maybe she would even get the first scoop of Purple Fluff (that's like ice cream for Unipegs)!

Unipeg and her parents trotted off to the recycling center, each pulling a big basket overflowing with cans and bottles.

Once they arrived, Unipeg emptied her baskets into the Big Counter, the machine that counted all your cans and bottles and then spat out the reward.

Click, clack, crash, went each can as it fell down the silver chute and landed in the pile of other cans and bottles. *Beep beep boop,* sputtered the Big Counter as it popped out Unipeg's reward.

"Look, Mom! Now I can get the toy," squeeled Unipeg happily.

Unipeg's heart raced as she galloped out of the recycling center. However, it was not long before they slowed to a trot. Outside it felt like the inside of an oven. Heat waves radiated from the ground. There was not a drop of water in sight. *Wheeeew, I'm glad I'll be at the pool party soon,* Unipeg thought. As Unipeg wondered which friend she would blast first with her Super-Duper-Splish-Splash-Blaster 3000, they passed an old, shaggy dog with its tongue sticking out. The dog was laying down, panting in the heat. His fur smelled like old, dirty gym socks. Next to the dog was a cardboard sign that said, "Thirsty Dog. No Home. No Friends. Need Help."

Unipeg paused and looked at the thirsty dog.

"What does it mean, 'No home,' Momma? Everyone should have a home, especially him. He needs to ask his parents for a bath!" said Unipeg.

Unipeg's mother smiled. "That's true, Unipeg, but some animals do not have homes, or bathtubs, or even soap and water."

"How come he has no water?" Unipeg asked her father.

"Some animals are not as lucky as we are, Unipeg. Sometimes, those animals need help," her father replied.

Unipeg wondered how she could help. She doubted that the dog would want her sparkly bow or sequin bathing suit, and she did not have any water with her. She knew, however, that on a hot day like today, everyone needs at least a drink of water and a place to cool off.

She shook her mane and out fell the sack of doubloons. She had worked so hard for this. If she gave these to the thirsty dog, then there would none left to use on the Super-Duper-Splash-Splash-Blaster 3000. She imagined arriving at the party without it. She imagined the disappointment of her friends. She imagined an empty pool with no toys and an empty bowl with no Purple Fluff. But did she *need* those things?

By the time they reached the shaggy dog, Unipeg had made up her mind. She walked up to the dog and said, "Here, this is for you," and handed him her reward. Her toy could wait, but this dog needed water now.

The thirsty dog looked up at her, his lips dry and cracked. In a shaky voice he said, "I think I should change my sign. Today I have a friend."

" Service to **others**
        is the rent you pay
for your room here on
earth."

-Muhammad Ali, American Boxer

" Though we see
        the **same** world,
we see it through
different eyes."

– Virginia Woolf, modernist writer

Discussion Questions

Pick a few of these to discuss together tonight. You don't have to complete everything now. It's just a list of options, so pick a few of your favorites!

1. Who is the most generous person you know? Why?
2. Where have you seen the most generous people?
3. What generous thing has someone done for you recently? How did you know they were being generous?
4. Do you have everything you want? Do you have everything you need?
5. What is one thing you are grateful for today?
6. If you had to donate part of your allowance or birthday money, where would you send it?
7. If you were sick or lonely what would you want others to do for you?
8. What do you do with old clothes, toys, books, games, or movies?
9. If you had to part with one item in your room right now, what would it be? Who would you give it to?
10. Would you rather give money or give time to something or someone you cared about?

10 Ways to Be More Generous. Have you done any of these?

1. Invite a friend over for dinner that you (helped) prepare.
2. Let your siblings borrow your toys, games, or art supplies.
3. Give someone a compliment.
4. Volunteer at a soup kitchen or participate in a food drive.
5. Participate with your parents in a charitable walk.
6. Create an exchange system where each time you purchase something new, you donate something old.
7. Set up a lemonade or cookie stand and donate the proceeds to charity.
8. Do Reverse Trick or Treat where you pass out candy to your neighbors.
9. Make a handmade gift for a friend instead of buying them a toy.
10. Plant a flower for an elderly person.

Unipeg's Just for Fun Activities

When Unipeg isn't out recycling or feeding animals at the community barn, she plays these games:

Horseback Rides

Unipeg's dad lets her ride on his back around the house. A good unicorn can respond to voice commands or tapping. Have your children adjust the speed by gently tapping your side, or have them use voice commands to control the direction of your motions (e.g., left, right, back, forward).

Room Racing

Find your fellow unicorns and Pegasus pals and race up the stairs to your bedroom or sprint down the hallway to the bathroom. The finish line might be your pillow, your doorknob, or your toothbrush. Sometimes letting little siblings have a head start is the generous thing to do.

Service Scavenger Hunt

You have probably had a scavenger hunt before where you look for or collect a list of items; this is a different kind of game. Instead of *taking* or *getting* items, you are *doing* different things for others.

Rules:

With the help of your parents, ask a few neighbors, relatives, or friends if they would like to participate in the Service Scavenger Hunt. Play this game by yourself or with others in teams.

Do not attempt to play the game with strangers or in places that you do not know. Service tasks should only be performed in areas you know and with people you trust. Younger children may need to be escorted during the game.

Once you have your participants, it is time to come up with a list of tasks that you and your teammates must accomplish. Here are a few suggestions:

- Rake leaves/shovel snow/pull weeds
- Empty dishwasher
- Vacuum for elderly
- Bake cookies and take them to a fire station
- Read a story to a child
- Collect 20 items for recycling
- Take out the garbage
- Feed a family pet, even when it's not your turn
- Water plants/garden
- Walk a neighborhood dog (with permission)
- Wash a car
- Pass out homemade cards in a nursing home

- Send a letter to our military overseas
- Pick up trash in a local park or community area

How to Play: Use the list above or create your own and set a time limit. As you do the tasks, check them off the list or take pictures as you complete each one. If you have multiple teams, the first team to complete the list wins!

I ATTRIBUTE MY **SUCCESS** TO THIS: I NEVER GAVE OR TOOK **any** EXCUSE.

Florence Nightingale,

founder of modern nursing

Determination

Everyday heroes are determined. Determination takes willpower and focus. Determined people have the patience to complete something from start to finish. They do not complain when things don't go as planned or when it's more work than expected. Determination is about doing something over and over again until you become better. It means not getting frustrated when you do not get it perfect the first time.

You need determination when you learn to bake a pizza from scratch. First, you roll out the dough. Without enough flour, it may stick to your roller or cooking pan. After waiting for the dough to rise, you have to decide if you want thick crust or thin crust. Sometimes, it takes more than one attempt to roll the dough just right. Next, you have to add the right amount of sauce. Don't forget the cheese and other toppings! You might need to experiment with a number of different combinations to get it just right. Even if you get hungry while making pizza, don't eat all the pepperoni slices. Then, you have to bake the pizza in the oven, but don't leave the kitchen just yet! It might burn. After the pizza comes out of the oven, you have to be patient and wait for it to cool down, or you might burn your mouth. Ouch! As you can see, it takes a lot of work and determination to make a tasty pizza.

Everyday heroes need determination to reach their final goals. You might fail the first time, the second time, and maybe even more—but that means next time you know what *not* to do. Determined heroes don't let anything hold them back from their dreams.

" The difference
.... between the **impossible**
and the possible lies in
a man's determination."

-Tommy Lasorda, American Baseball Legend

Joining the Band

The bad news was that The Amazing Milkers, Utty's favorite band, lost their lead guitarist, Jimmy Cowman. Cowman moved to Australia to focus on his acting career, starring in the movie, *I Love Moo*. The good news was that there were open auditions for a new lead guitarist!

Utty, an 8-year old cow, had taken music lessons for the past three years. Although he was talented, he did not like to practice. His mother reminded him to practice after dinner every night, but he always wiggled out of it with funny excuses and complaints that his hooves were too sore.

One day Utty came home from school with exciting news. "Mom, guess what!" Utty exclaimed, jumping up and down next to her.

"What is it?" asked his mother with a curious grin.

"The Amazing Milkers are holding tryouts for a new lead guitarist! And they will be coming to Dairyville Colliseum in three months," replied Utty.

"Fantastic! Will you try out for the spot?" asked his mother.

"You bet, mom! I am going to be the next Amazing Milker rock star!" exclaimed Utty as he spun in a circle with a wide air guitar motion.

"Utty, I heard that you are auditioning for the Amazing Milkers," said his father at breakfast the next morning. "I hope you realize how much practice it will require to learn all of their songs."

"Practice!? Oh Dad, I already know all their songs. They are my favorite band!" said Utty. He began listing all the songs in his head. Utty paused mid-mouthful-of-cereal and thought about how many Amazing Milkers songs he could *actually* play.

He could *sing* most of them, but he could only play a couple of their most recent hits. Most of his guitar practice had been on the classics like "The Rocking Roosters" and "Piggelicious."

"Maybe I could use a little more practice, but I have three whole months," Utty finally said confidently.

"What do *you* think the Amazing Milkers do when they are not performing, Utty?" asked his father.

"Probably going to big parties, signing autographs, getting their picture taken, staying up late, eating Purple Fluff…" Utty said merrily, imagining what life would be like as a rock star.

"When do you think they practice?" asked his father.

"Maybe a little before they go on stage. They don't need lots of practice. They are rock stars!" replied Utty.

"Even professionals practice. How else could they perform so well?" said Utty's father.

Hmm, thought Utty. "I thought the Amazing Milkers were just born that good."

"Remember Utty, we practice before we play," said Utty's father as he gave Utty a pat on the back.

On the way home from school the next day, Utty's friends asked him to join them at the new roller skating park in town. "I can't, guys," said Utty. "I have to practice guitar."

"Ah cowpies, that stinks. You're gonna miss out!" said his friends. But Utty thought to himself: *Practice before play.* He had many songs to learn.

The next week there was a big pizza party at the neighbor's house and all the cool cows would be there.

"Come on, Utty! Can't you come over just this once? Practice tomorrow; skipping one day of practicing won't hurt," called his friends.

It was hard to say no. Eating pizza and staying up late watching movies with friends was way more fun than practicing. Utty *had* already learned half of the songs. Maybe skipping one day would not matter. Then he imagined the callback list without his name on it. If he could not play all the songs perfectly he might not make it.

"Dudes, I really want to, but if I don't play these songs perfectly, then I might not make it in the band," he said.

Utty practiced every afternoon, weekday and weekend. As his friends played and wrestled outside, he rocked out to the guitar solo in "Moovin' On Over" and played "Dairy Girl" perfectly for the first time.

Three months later…

"Utty, you put a lot of work into this audition. Your mom and I are very proud. We hope you do well, son," said Utty's father with a proud grin.

"Thanks, Mom and Dad. That really means a lot. I can't imagine how tired you are of hearing the same songs, but I really appreciate you listening and telling me where I needed to improve. Wish me luck!"

Utty trotted into the building and went straight for the audition schedule. His eyes scrolled down the list and to his surprise he was listed last. There were *nineteen* other guitarists in front of him. He was disappointed, but he had waited weeks to try out. He could wait a few more hours.

While Utty listened to the other guitar players, he heard many of them struggle on the less popular songs. *That's what I used to sound like. I guess that's what happens when you go to the park and eat pizza instead of practicing,* thought Utty. *Practice over play.*

The loud speaker finally called his name, "Utty Mooten, it is time for your audition." Utty trotted confidently into the room. The band members had their instruments out and the managers had pencils and scoring cards. As he plugged his fierce red and orange electric guitar into the amp, Rocky Moodell, the lead singer said, "Let's hear what you got, little dude."

Utty cranked up the volume on his amp and played their current number one radio hit, "Milkshake Quake." He played the first part of the song just as written, but put his own twist on the guitar solo in the second part. The band members were stomping their hooves and playing right along with him, but it was only at the end of the song that Utty realized the band had jumped in. Rocky could not hide the smile from his face.

"Utty, that rocked! You were incredible, man!" he said.

Next, the Milkers asked Utty to play some of their less popular songs. Although many of the earlier guitarists struggled with these, Utty's hooves glided effortlessly from string to string, song to song. After a quick discussion with the manager, each of the band members walked up and shook Utty's hand.

When Rocky finally reached him, he said, "Utty, expect a call next week. We think you would be a great addition to our band." Utty's legs turned to butter. He was finally a rock star!

"You have to .... **expect** things of yourself before you can do them."

-Michael Jordan, American Basketball Player

" A journey of .... a **thousand** miles begins with a single step."

-Laozi, Chinese Philosopher, from Tao Te Ching

Discussion Questions

Pick a few of these to discuss together tonight. You don't have to complete everything now. It's just a list of options, so pick a few of your favorites!

1. In the story, what was Utty's goal?
2. What are some of your goals?
3. Why was Utty so determined to practice?
4. What do you love to practice? What do you NOT love to practice?
5. What is one of the hardest activities for you to complete?
6. How did you feel after you finished that activity?
7. When was the last time struggled with something? Were you by yourself or in front of others?
8. When is the last time you did something without struggling?
9. Have you ever seen me (your parent) struggle? What did I do to overcome my struggle?
10. Who helps you stay committed to something when you feel like giving up?

10 Ways to Be More Determined. Have you done any of these?

1. Make goals.
2. Are passionate about something.
3. Practice your skills and activities, even if you don't want to.
4. Learn from your mistakes.
5. Never give up on the first try.
6. Don't let excuses or other obstacles get in your way.
7. Ignore distractions.
8. Never stop before you give your best to complete the goal.
9. Don't give into peer pressure or let others bring you down.
10. Don't take the "easy way" out in every situation.

Utty's Just for Fun Activities

Utty is now busy practicing for his next performance, but even rock stars can have fun! These are the games he likes to play when he's on the tour bus:

Hide and Go Seek

No explanation needed here. Select your count, find your hiding places, and have fun. For the more advanced hide and go seekers, you can add a blindfold to the searcher, and have the hiders offer three claps for the seeker (Hide and Go Clap).

Tic Tac Toe

A classic with the kids and cows alike. X O X O, object is to get three in a row.

Driving Me Bananas!

In this interactive game, everyday heroes learn about teamwork and creativity along with practice, patience, and determination.

Have heroes line up or create a circle. The object of this game is to pass a banana (or another oddly shaped fruit, vegetable, or toy) around *without* using your hands.

You need to get creative and plan your next move. Maybe the first person grabs it with their armpit, then the next with elbows, then knees, etc. Carefully plan and practice the next move while patiently waiting your turn.

Encourage heroes to see how long they can pass the item without dropping it.

YOU

ARE THE *designer*
OF YOUR OWN DESTINY...
THE **pen** IS IN YOUR HAND, AND THE
OUTCOME IS WHATEVER YOU *choose*.

Lisa Nichols
From Rhonda Byrne's The Secret (2006)

Creativity

Everyday heroes are creative. Have you ever heard the phrase, "When life gives you lemons, you make lemonade?" Even when unexpected or disappointing events occur, the creative person figures out another way to succeed. Everyday heroes believe in a solution to every problem, even though it might not be obvious at first.

Creative everyday heroes know that sometimes their ideas might not work, but they try it out anyway. Everyday heroes are creative when they have to make a new type of sandwich because they are all out of peanut butter and jelly. An everyday hero might have to create a fun game for their siblings during a long car ride.

Creativity helps us discover new things. Everyday heroes are game changers. They are not afraid to think differently than others or try a new approach if it means that they might create something better.

Creative everyday heroes are flexible. They do not give up when everything they expected fails to happen. Creativity requires a healthy imagination and confidence in your ideas. Everyday heroes save the day when people think the situation is hopeless. They show creativity when they solve problems in original ways that help others.

"**Necessity** *is the* ·················
·········· *mother of invention.*"

—Jonathan Swift, Anglo-Irish Satirist, Essayist

One Bear's Trash is Another Scout's Treasure

Cupcake, the pure white polar bear cub, was a proud member of the Anchorage Alaska Bear Scouts. Over the past few months, she earned bear badges for skills like archery, berry identification, knot tying, and picnic basket weaving, just to name a few. Scouts needed at least twenty badges to go on a camping trip, and finally Cupcake and her friends had enough. This was her very first camping trip. Friday after school, her scout group headed for the East Fork Trail and Tulchina Falls.

The rain started as soon as they arrived at camp. Cupcake and her fellow scouts did not mind though, a little rain never bothered any bear. They loved mud puddle stomping and playing mud tag. (The best part was that no one had to take baths afterward!)

Late Saturday afternoon it was *still* raining. Mrs. Beary, the scout leader, sent Cupcake and three others up the mountain to gather supplies at the resupply hut. Cupcake volunteered to lead the hike so she could practice her navigation. The hike was not too hard, but the wooden bridges were slippery when wet.

Higher up in the mountain, it seemed they had hiked right into the middle of the storm. Thunder clapped and lightening flashed angrily around them making their bear hairs stand straight up. The trails were washing away, and each step sent the bears slipping and sliding. Cupcake decided to turn her troop around and try again later. It just was not safe to hike right now.

The bears quickly scampered down the mountain until they reached the bridge…or at least, the pile of broken wood that was *once* a bridge. Oh no! The creek (now a raging river) had destroyed the flimsy bridge.

"Uh oh, Cupcake, what are we going to do? How will we get back to camp?" Jolly said fearfully.

"Cupcake, I'm scared," cried Tulip as she looked up at the darkening sky. Soon it would turn black. "That bridge was the only crossing, and the water is moving way too fast to swim across."

Cupcake marched back and forth, thinking hard. *This is a* real *problem,* she thought. The murky water whizzed and whirled like an angry, liquid tornado. Tulip was right. They could not swim across and it was getting late. Would they have to spend the night out in the cold rain? Then, something caught her eye. *That doesn't belong in the creek,* thought Cupcake.

It was no longer only fish, sticks, and leaves floating in the creek. Bobbing up and down were wet balls of rope, soggy honey sandwiches, slippery steel tent poles, and *lots* of plastic bags. *Those look like the materials from the resupply hut. Maybe they washed down from the top of the mountain,* thought Cupcake.

It probably isn't the only thing that's destroyed, sighed Cupcake thinking about how soaked her tent and sleeping bag must be by now. The bigger problem was crossing this river before dark. So far, no one had any ideas.

"We will *never* get out of here! It's hopeless," said Sprinkle as she plopped down into a muddy puddle in front of a tree. "We

are stuck in the woods by ourselves with *no* shelter, *no* map, and *no* honey to eat."

"I can't stand this rain. I can't stand camping any more. I want to go home!" yelled Jolly, stomping her feet.

"Wait, wait! We can't give up now! We're Bear Scouts! Remember last year when we won Best Recipe at the Annual Salmon Cooking Contest?" asked Cupcake.

"Yeah, I guess," said Sprinkle half-heartedly, scratching her back against a leaning tree.

"I remember!" said Tulip proudly.

"Sure, but how does that help us, Cupcake? There are no salmon contests out here in the woods," said Jolly, always skeptical.

"Do you remember *how* we won? It was our first time cooking salmon, and we were the youngest contestants. We won because we stuffed it with raspberries and smeared it with honey. No one had ever done that before!" said Cupcake. She took a step toward the creek and immediately stepped on a soggy sandwich that went *squish* under her toes.

"Ugh! Gross. This trash from the resupply hut is everywhere! What can we…wait a minute," Cupcake said slowly, an idea forming in her little bear brain. "We can turn this trash into treasure. We will use these supplies to build something. Grab everything you can!"

The bears quickly grabbed pawfuls of plastic bags, a handful of hiking rope, a tire, and a ton of metal tent poles. Only Sprinkle picked up the soggy sandwiches and licked the honey from between the slices of bread. "Sprinkle, those sandwiches are soggy. Yuck!" they all laughed. But without any dinner, Sprinkle was a very hungry bear.

Back by the leaning tree, they all counted their supplies. "What are we going to do with all of this?" they asked each other.

Cupcake smiled, "I have an idea. First, we will create a lasso using the rope. Then, we will use the tent poles to help us hook the lasso on the large stump across the river. The rope is too heavy to throw across the river by itself, and we can't risk dropping the rope in the water."

"I don't get it," said Jolly, confused.

"See that leaning tree. That branch reaches almost half way across the water. If we can connect five of the tent poles together, we can use the one long pole to slip the hiking rope onto that big stump across the water."

"How will we tie it to the stump, Cupcake? That's impossible," said a frustrated Tulip.

"Easy," said Cupcake, "I'll use the Tautline Hitch I learned to earn my knot tying badge. It slides and tightens without letting go, which is just what we need!"

Excited by Cupcake's plan, the bears quickly got to work.

"Look! I call it an extendo-pole!" laughed Sprinkle as she handed Cupcake the super long tent pole.

After Cupcake tied the rope, Jolly wrapped it around the extended tent pole, with the Tautline Hitch hanging freely at the end.

Quick as a flash of lightening, Cupcake climbed the tree and the other bears handed her the extendo-pole. It took a few tries, but Cupcake was finally able to reach the stump and slip the rope around it.

Cupcake pulled hard on the rope, and just as expected, the rope fastened securely around the tree stump. Cupcake tied the rope to the leaning tree and each bear shimmied across the rope and over the swirling water.

Cupcake was the last to cross and when she got down from the rope there was thunderous applause. "Your plan worked! We're alive! You really did it, Cupcake!" cried the bears.

"*We* did it…together," said Cupcake.

" You see things;

and you say, 'why?'
But I dream things that
never were; and I say,
'why not?'"

- George Bernard Shaw, playwright

" ...Everyone

is born with genius,
but some people only
keep it for a few
minutes. That is the
demand – to keep it."

-Martha Graham, quoting composer, Edgar Varese

Discussion Questions

Pick a few of these to discuss together tonight. You don't have to complete everything now. It's just a list of options, so pick a few of your favorites!

1. What was the bears' plan to cross the river?
2. What would you do differently?
3. Why was Cupcake creative in this story?
4. When is the last time you did something creative? What was it? Who was with you?
5. Do you like to come up with creative names, stories, crafts, or foods? What are some of your most recent creations?
6. If you had to build a boat from items in your bedroom, what would you choose to use?
7. If you went on a weekend camping trip, what three things would you pack first?
8. When you build a toy or bake something do you like to follow the instructions or recipe, or do you like to create your own?
9. Are you more creative by yourself or when you are in a group?
10. If you could create the best toy in the world, what would it be? Could you draw a picture of it?

10 Ways to Be More Creative. Would you describe yourself as any of these?

1. Not afraid to do things differently than others.
2. Love to create and invent new things
3. Enjoy building or putting things together.
4. Curious about the world around you.
5. Have lots of ideas and do your best to turn those ideas into realities!
6. Won't always go with the obvious choice.
7. An observer and daydreamer.
8. Seeker of new experiences.
9. Like to express yourself in a variety of ways (art, music, dance, poetry, etc.).
10. Know how to be creative even when there are lots of rules.

Cupcake's Just for Fun Activities

When Cupcake isn't out hiking, camping, and making bear crafts, she loves to play these games:

Build a Pillow and Blanket Fort

Grab a bunch of pillows and blankets and build a monster fort. Cupcake uses couches, food trays, tables, etc. to create the perfect fort. Don't forget your flashlight if you turn off the lights!

Build a House of Cards

When Cupcake can't get the house too dirty, she builds a house of cards instead of a fort. She grabs a deck of playing cards and builds a structure out of them. For more advanced builders: try making your structure wind-proof from the occasional Dad/Mom hurricane.

Weird Dinner Night

Have some fun with your children by cooking up some unusual food. Here are some ideas to get you started:

1. Choose an item from the grocery store that you have never cooked with or eaten.
2. Cook something without using a recipe.
3. Make something just using only what you have at home already.
4. Choose a color theme for the food (for example, "yellow night": cornmeal, yellow peppers, bananas, etc.)
5. Use food coloring to make things different colors (e.g., royal purple milk, baby blue bread, powder pink butter, grassy green eggs and ham, ruby red macaroni and cheese, etc.).
6. Switch flavors. Try making sweet things taste sour (for example, putting balsamic vinegar on your ice cream.)
7. Choose one food that has to be in every dish (for example, bacon!)
8. For St. Patrick's day, green is often the favorite color. For Halloween, orange and black usually win out. For Easter, yellow and pink take first prize. For all other days, anything goes.
9. Backwards dinner night! (Dessert-Dinner-Appetizers)
10. Tea Time (scones, cucumber sandwiches, and cookies) or Breakfast for Dinner

IF YOUR ACTIONS **inspire** OTHERS TO **dream** MORE, LEARN MORE, DO MORE, AND BECOME MORE, YOU ARE A **leader**.

John Quincy Adams,

6th U.S. President

Leadership

Everyday heroes are not afraid to be leaders when the time is right. You do not have to be the president of the United States, a chief executive officer of a company, a firefighter, a police officer, or a military general to be a leader. Leaders are not always "in command."

Sometimes a leader is just the first person to try something new, lend a helping hand to someone else, or volunteer for the job no one else wants to do. People can be leaders in class, at sports camp, during scout meetings, or even at a friend's house. Everyday heroes can be leaders by taking action when others hesitate or choose to do nothing at all.

Many people want to be leaders, yet they think they are too shy, too young, or too inexperienced. Maybe leadership means that you take the lead role in your school play, sign up as a volunteer at local community group, or invite the new kid to sit at your lunch table. Everyday heroes take the lead even on the little things like chores or class activities.

You can even practice leadership by helping *others* lead. Leaders do not need to be popular, powerful, or even *the best*. Leaders might assign duties to the group so that everyone can participate. Leaders have a positive attitude and keep up the group morale. As an everyday hero, you can be a leader for your family, for your siblings, or even your friends. Leaders give people confidence and make a difference in other people's lives.

" Ultimately, leadership requires **action**: daring to take steps that are **necessary** but unpopular, challenging the status quo in order to reach a **brighter** future."

-Benazir Bhutto, Pakistan's Prime Minister, first woman to lead a Muslim state.

The New Pup

Spots woke up today without an alarm clock. Today was the day he had waited for all year: HIS BIRTHDAY! He looked outside – sunny, warm, perfect. His parents were already outside setting up picnic tables for ice cream and a doggy bounce house for Spots and his friends. It was not every day a pup turned two years old (14 in human years).

Spots' school friends were the first to arrive: Sammy Shepard, Donny Doberman, Lonna Lab, and Polly Palmaranian.

"Hey guys, come on out back," Spots barked from the door.

The tight group of puppy pals all ran straight for the doggy bounce house and started jumping and sliding. Each doggie took a turn flipping, rolling, and making funny poses. They all begged Lonna, a cheerleader, to show off her back flip. She always made it look easy.

Bobby Bulldog arrived last to the party. As soon as Spots saw him, he bounced off instantly, but his friends were not ready to stop playing.

"Ah bones, Spots. I was about to show everyone my back flip!" whined Lonna.

"Yeah, who is *that*, Spots?" snipped Sammy. He didn't really like new dogs, but Spots wasted no time introducing Bobby to each of his friends.

"Bobby, I'm so glad you could make it. This is Sammy, Donny, Lonna, and Polly. We go to Barksdale Elementary School together."

"Hi Bobby," said Polly and Donny politely. Lonna and Sammy were not as excited about this new visitor.

"You look pretty small to be in Spots' grade," said Lonna with smirk. Bobby immediately felt embarrassed.

Seeing how uncomfortable Bobby looked, Spots chimed in, "He might be small, but this doggie can jump! It's pretty cool."

"Really?" asked Sammy. "How do you know he can do that?"

"I met Spots at camp," said Bobby quietly.

"We played on the same soccer team," said Spots proudly as he dribbled a soccer ball across the yard.

"Spots was the one who taught me how to play goalie," said Bobby shyly.

"Really? I'm a goalie too!" said Polly with excitement. "I'm not very good though, and we *never* have two goalies at school."

"You *must* be pretty good if you can play soccer with *Spots*," said Lonna snobbishly. "He's the best player in the league right now."

"Why don't we play a game right now," said Spots.

"I'm not so sure, Spots. The little guy will probably get hurt playing with us big dogs," said Lonna. Lonna was stubborn and always wanted her way.

"We'll see about that," Spots said with paws up towards Bobby. "Bobby, don't go easy on them!"

"I want Bobby on *my* team!" yipped Polly. "No way, he's on *my* team," Donny barked.

Everyone laughed, but Bobby was glowing. He was never the first one to be picked on a team. He felt like he had super-doggie strength.

"Bobby will be on my team. Lonna too," said Spots. "Polly, you play the other goalie with Donny and Sammy."

"I remember when my brothers first played soccer with me. I think I was probably even smaller than Bobby," Donny told Spots as they walked out to the yard.

"Yeah, I guess it is tough being the little guy," agreed Sammy.

"We all need to give him a chance. I think he could be on our soccer team someday," said Spots.

As Donny and Sammy were getting ready to start the game, Spots winked at both of them: "Let's help Bobby show his stuff. He is just starting to kick the ball around. Nobody starts out as an all-star athlete, but we can help him gain a little confidence."

On the field, Bobby was the star. His small size did not keep him from heroically diving for the ball with his paws. By the end of the game, Bobby was part of the crew. Tongue out and tail wagging, Bobby got a paw bump from every teammate, even Lonna.

"I didn't think you could play, but Spots was right. You are great!" said Lonna.

When it was time for birthday cake Bobby wiggled into the seat next to Spots.

"Thanks for sticking up for me back there, Spots. I had a lot of fun once we started playing," he said.

"You really showed your stuff out there. I knew you had it in you!" barked Spots happily. "I hope I see you on the field again soon...on *my* team."

" A **leader** ⋯⋯⋯⋯⋯⋯⋯⋯
⋯⋯⋯ takes people where
they want to go. A great
leader takes people where
they don't necessarily
want to go, but ought to be."

-Rosalynn Carter, first lady to 39th U.S. President

"Don't follow ⋯⋯⋯⋯⋯⋯
⋯⋯⋯ the **crowd**, let the
crowd follow you."

-Margaret Thatcher, British Prime Minister

Spot's Just for Fun Activities

When Spot's isn't leading team practice or just kicking a ball around, he likes to play these games:

Red Light/Green Light

This is a follow-the-leader type game where one person leads the rest. The caller or leader calls red light for stop, green light for go. Don't get caught moving when someone calls "Red light!"

Thumb Wars

Lock hands and battle away with your thumbs. Classic battle cry at the beginning of each battle: "One, two, three, four, I declare a thumb war!" Even leaders don't win every one of these battles!

Discussion Questions

Pick a few of these to discuss together tonight. You don't have to complete everything now. It's just a list of options, so pick a few of your favorites!

1. Who was the leader in this story? Why?
2. Who was NOT a leader in this story? Why?
3. Have you ever attended a party where you didn't know anyone? Did you have a friend like Spots to help you?
4. Can you remember the last time you needed a leader?
5. When do you like being a leader?
6. If you were going to a new place, who would you want to bring you around? Why?
7. How would you expect a leader to treat you or others?
8. What kind of activities require leadership?
9. Can you name an activity that requires leadership?
10. What could you do to show that you are a leader?

10 Ways to Be a Leader. Have you done any of these?

1. Taught someone something you know
2. Served as the leader or spokesperson of your class
3. Helped a friend or sibling with their homework
4. Asked questions in class
5. Made a meal for your family
6. Led an activity or practice with your group or team
7. Volunteered your time
8. Helped others achieve their goals
9. Been asked for advice or help
10. Encouraged others to lead

Leadership Committee

Who's on Your Leadership Committee?

Imagine you have a problem you need to solve or a project you need to lead. You might need to come up with an idea for the science fair, throw a surprise party for your best friend, replace a missing teammate for the next sports season ahead, or organize a decorating crew for a charity event.

You gather five trusted committee members at your "discussion table" to help you solve this problem or plan for this event. Who would be at this table with you? Who are the great leaders and role models in your life? Whose table would you be at? Who looks up to you as a leader, or who do you hope looks up to you?

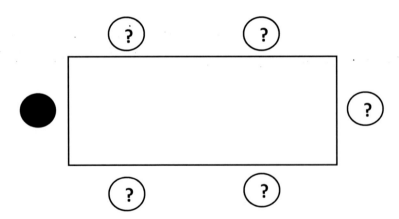

IN **any** MOMENT OF DECISION, THE BEST THING YOU CAN DO IS THE **right** THING, THE NEXT BEST THING YOU CAN DO IS THE **wrong** THING, THE WORST THING YOU COULD DO IS **nothing**.

Theodore Roosevelt, 26th U.S. President

Responsibility

People trust everyday heroes. Have you ever told someone a secret? Did you tell someone who gossips about others or did you tell someone you trust? Have you ever invited a friend to the zoo or museum? Did you invite someone who would show up on time and be ready or someone who forgets their ticket or their lunch? We trust responsible people—people who do the right thing and keep their promises. Despite popular belief, responsible people are not perfect. Not even Superman is perfect! But when everyday heroes break a promise or do something wrong, they make up for it.

Everyday heroes are accountable. If something happens, they take ownership of the consequences. If they forget to do their homework, they do not blame the dog. When an everyday hero tells you they will participate in a lemonade stand, work on a school science project, or help you wash a car, they keep their promises.

Why should everyday heroes be responsible? Life is full of choices. To make the right decision, you must think about the consequences of the choices you make. Consequences are the natural result of good choices and bad choices, of meeting or not meeting your responsibilities. When you receive a zero on your homework because you did not do it, it is not because the teacher does not like you. It is because you made the decision not to do it.

Everyday heroes do not blame others. They know that other people and circumstances are not responsible for what happens to them. Instead of acting like the victim, heroes accept the consequences and make the change.

" *I believe* that it's in your moments of **decision** that your destiny is shaped."

-Tony Robbins, from Unlimited Power (1986)

Breakfast Bonanza

"You cannot escape the responsibility of tomorrow by evading it today."

-Abraham Lincoln, 16th U.S. President

Crack! went the egg. *Sizzle! Splat!* went the butter in a hot pan. Sunny's ears perked up. The scent of spicy sausage and sweet, maple syrup pancakes crept up the stairs and into Sunny's bedroom. Sunny's nose prickled. *Mmm,* she thought. Sunny woke up every weekend to those sounds. Rain or shine, her parents always made Sunny this special breakfast on Saturday and Sunday. She called these weekend morning meals "Breakfast Bonanzas." Those were the best days of the week, according to Sunny.

Sunny's parents already had a plate of pancakes ready for her as she bounced down the stairs.

"You know how I know you love me, Mommy and Daddy?" asked Sunny, as she flipped a flapjack into her floppy mouth.

"How?" asked Sunny's mommy, dusting the next pancake with powdered sugar.

"Because you never miss a Breakfast Bonanza," said Sunny, with sticky syrup all over her paws and a super wide smile.

Saturdays also happened to be chore days. These were not as much fun as sausages, pancakes, and maple syrup. After slurping down her last greasy sausage link, she looked at her chore list:

CHORE LIST	
Clean bedroom	
Pick up toys and games	✓
Empty wastebaskets	✓
Clean guinea pig cage	
Food and water for guinea pig	
Empty dishwasher	✓

"Argh, this will take me *at least* an hour!" whined Sunny.

This particular Saturday was the big, annual DogHunt game day and she was on a team with her five pug buds. The game started in just under an hour down at the park.

"I have to be there for my team!" she crired.

"I'm sorry, Sunny, but you know chores come before play," said Daddy, as he cut into his sausage and pancakes.

Sunny growled and started collecting the wastebaskets. After she shoved all her mess under her bed and dumped the wastebaskets outside, she looked at her Guinea pig cage.

Hmmm, the cage doesn't smell that *bad,* Sunny thought. *And there is plenty of water for today. I'll just feed her when I get back. Mommy and Daddy won't mind and probably won't check until later!*

Deciding to save the Guinea Pig for later, Sunny sprinted down the stairs. Mommy was at the door, ready to give Sunny her water bottle.

"Thank you for doing your chores, Sunny," she said sweetly. "We all have to pitch in sometimes."

Sunny felt a little guilty for not doing *all* her chores. *I'll do them eventually*, she told herself. "Love you, Mommy. See you tonight!" she barked.

After the game of DogHunt, Sunny's friends invited her out to dinner and a movie. Her best friend's parents offered to drive all of them to see the new movie *Doglight*, a story about a young dog who falls in love with a vampire dog. Sunny could not pass that up!

She came home a little later than expected, only a few minutes before bedtime. She almost fell asleep on the fuzzy carpet floor in front of her bed. *I'm soooo tired*, she said to herself. Sunny went straight to bed without even changing into her pajamas.

When Sunny woke up the next morning, she did not hear the usual sounds of cracking eggs or sizzling butter. *I wonder what time it is*, thought Sunny. *Maybe it's still too early.* However, her red flashing alarm clock read: 9:47 A.M.

Wait, it's already morning? wondered Sunny. She rushed down the stairs to find her parents already cleaning up the breakfast dishes.

"Mommy, where are the pancakes and sausage?" asked Sunny with a wide yawn. There must be some mistake.

"Oh. Daddy and I just decided to have some eggs this morning," said Mommy, carefully washing a bowl.

"But what about our Breakfast Bonanza?" asked Sunny, now confused.

"We did not feel like doing all that extra work this morning. Actually, Mommy and I are about to go to the beach instead. Grandma said she would watch you until we return," said Daddy from the living room.

"But…but what about me? What about *my* breakfast?" asked Sunny, her tummy grumbling.

"We figured you could make something yourself. Oatmeal is on the top shelf," said Mommy, looking at Daddy across the way.

"But I can't reach the top shelf! I'm too small to do it on my own," cried Sunny, her tummy growling like a grizzly bear.

"We know you will figure it out. We are leaving for the beach, sweetheart. If you need anything, grandma is out back in the garden. We will be back in time for dinner," said Daddy.

"DINNER!? I am hungry *now*! Please! It's your job to feed me," Sunny barked.

"Oh, did you hear that, Daddy? It is our job to feed Sunny. Why is it our job if you are the one who is hungry?" asked Mommy softly.

"Because…because you are my parents and you promised to take care of me forever," replied Sunny.

"You know, that's right, Mommy. We did promise to feed Sunny, buy her treats, and take care of her no matter what other fun things *we* wanted to do instead," said Daddy.

"Yes, I remember now," said Mommy. "I also remember a little puppy that made a promise to take care of her pet guinea pig…"

Sunny's hunger suddenly disappeared and her heart sunk as she remembered her poor little pet.

"Oh no...I forgot to feed the guinea pig last night. I'm supposed to be her Mommy," said Sunny looking at the cage.

"She would have gone to bed with no breakfast *or* dinner last night. Even worse, her water bottle was empty. She was probably just as hungry and thirsty as you are right now," said Mommy.

Sunny walked over to the guinea pig cage and picked up the tiny fur-ball creature. "I'm so sorry," she said to the guinea pig. "This morning, *you* are getting a Breakfast Bonanza!"

"You cannot control ········ what happens to you in life, but you can always **control** what you will feel and do about what **happens** to you."

-Viktor E. Frankl, from Man's Search for Meaning

"You'll **always** miss ········ 100% of the shots you don't take."

—Wayne Gretzky, Hockey Legend

Discussion Questions

Pick a few of these to discuss together tonight. You don't have to complete everything now. It's just a list of options, so pick a few of your favorites!

1. Why was it not responsible of Sunny to go play a game before feeding her Guinea pig?
2. Can you still be responsible if you sometimes forget to do the things you promised someone?
3. What would you do if you forgot to feed your pet or if you forgot to bring a present to a friend's birthday party?
4. What would you do if you make two different commitments on the same day like Sunny?
5. What responsibilities do you have at home? At school?
6. What happens when you don't do what you are supposed to do at home or at school?
7. What do you do to help you remember your responsibilities?
8. If you were able to make the rules and assign chores at home, what would be the rules for your parents? Your siblings?
9. What would you do if someone forgot to do something you assigned?
10. What if you got in trouble because someone forgot to do their part? What would you say to them?

10 Ways to Be More Responsible. Have you done any of these?

1. Picked up trash at the park or on a trail.
2. Helped someone find something that was lost.
3. Cleaned up after yourself at home or at a friend's house.
4. Written a thank you note.
5. Cleared the table without being asked.
6. Volunteered to stay after school and help a teacher with something.
7. Turned something into the lost and found instead of taking it.
8. Told the truth, even when there would be consequences.
9. Obeyed your bedtime rules, even when you have a babysitter.
10. Ate your vegetables, even when they weren't your favorite.

Match the opposites:

"I'm the one responsible."	Breaking a promise
Truth	Quit
Making a commitment	Last to volunteer
Give	Discourage
First to volunteer	Lie
Finish	Take
Encourage	"It's your fault!"

Sunny's Just for Fun Activities

Sunny loves to play games almost as much as she likes playing DogHunt. After she finishes her chores, she plays these games with her parents:

Pick a Board Game

Pick a favorite board game, or choose one you have not played in a long time. All that matters is the family time.

Tooth Brush Racing

Compete in the tooth brushing world championship. Each night, Sunny and her dad race to the bathroom to get to the toothpaste and start their electric brushes. Since they both have the identical three-minute timer, getting to the toothpaste first is critical to winning the race. Although her dad can try to shut off his toothbrush early, Sunny is onto his clever ways!

Alternative races include picking up the most toys and matching the most socks.

The Blindfold Challenge

Can YOU make it to safety?

In order to play this game, first choose a "safe zone." It could be the house, a tree, or any other place.

Round 1:

1. The parent puts on the blindfold.
2. The child helps the blindfolded parent reach the final destination.

Round 2:

1. Swap the blindfold so your child can experience the feeling of being led.
2. The parent helps the blindfolded child reach the final destination.

The mission of this game is to get everyone to the "safe zone." Will you do it by holding hands, using verbal commands, putting your hands on their shoulders, making weird noises, using one clap straight and two claps right and three claps left? Be creative, but don't let anyone get hurt!

Many OF LIFE'S FAILURES ARE PEOPLE WHO DID NOT REALIZE HOW close THEY WERE TO **success** WHEN THEY GAVE UP.

Thomas Edison, American inventor

Resilience

Everyday heroes are resilient. When everyday heroes meet an obstacle in the road, they figure out a way around it. When life pushes them down, they bounce back. But get this: even everyday heroes mess up. They fail tests, break bones, miss the bus, get embarrassed, and struggle with friendships. There will be mistakes, failure, and loss in our lives. Sometimes it's our fault, other times it's not. However, everyday heroes know that it's all about the attitude.

We all handle emotions and practice resilience in different ways. Some of us write or doodle in a journal. Others may go for a run or ride their bike. Still others pray or play a musical instrument. Some people have a secret hideout where they go to find strength; others have a special friend with whom they can share their feelings.

Sometimes there won't be someone to protect us from challenges. Life is not always comfortable and we do not always get our way. Everyday heroes do not expect help all the time. Part of resilience is problem solving. When failure or loss happens, you must change your perspective and bring it back into your control. Do not be afraid of loss or risk, find a way to learn and grow from it.

On days where you feel like nothing goes right, remember what you *are* good at, why people *do* love you, and things that *do* get you excited. Everyday heroes are like rubber bands. Situations or people may stretch them, and sometimes that stretching is uncomfortable, but everyday heroes know how to spring back before they snap.

"I can **accept** failure—everyone fails at something. But I can't accept not trying."

-Michael Jordan, American basketball star

The Biggest Game of the Year

" Never give up! Failure and rejection are only the first step to succeeding!"

—Jim Valvano, American basketball coach

Ready or not, here it was: Game Day. Spots had heard the rumors: "All the United dogs weigh over 100 pounds!" "They have paws the size of dinner plates!" He was nervous, but he didn't need to be.

His team, the Canine Revolution, had finished the regular season 12-0. Spots was the team captain and striker. His best friend Donny Doberman was co-captain and fellow forward. They were both all-stars. Everyone at school knew their names and the local newspaper, *The Doggytown Times*, recorded every detail of their winning streak. On and off the field, they were invincible. The coach often complimented Donny and Spots on mastering the use of the long ball and aggressive diagonal runs behind the opposing team's defenders. Last week's sports section cover story read: "The unbeatable team wins again after Doggie Duo, "Splash and Dash" (Spots and Donny), scored a perfect last minute goal. No one can stop the offensive tidal wave of the Canine Revolution!"

Camera lights flashed as Spots slowly walked onto the soccer field. The howling crowd echoed from the walls of the stadium. Spots was excited to see his parents in the stands, along with his grandparents, and friends from his birthday party. He could hear everyone cheering for his team: *"Have a great game, Spots!"* and *"Bring home the gold, Revolution!"* and *"Hustle hard, Canines."*

113

Spots spent weeks practicing for this game, and knew in his heart that it would be his best game ever. With so many friends and family in the stands, he couldn't ask for a better set-up for helping his team win the state championship. Although he was nervous, this was no time to get cold paws.

"All right, Revolution, bring it in!" barked coach Rottweiler. "You have worked long and hard this season to get to the state championship. Today is the day we show our fans and the rest of the league our skills. No matter what happens on this field today, the entire town is proud of you. Let's win this one, boys! On three, I want to hear everyone yell *Revolution*…ONE, TWO, THREE, *REVOLUTION*," cried coach Rottweiler and all of the Revolution players.

Spots and Donny sprinted to center field for the coin toss. Donny and Spots always called heads. As the coin spun in the air, their stomachs spun too. Today, luck was on their side. Canine Revolution would start with the ball.

From the first touch, the game was a flurry of activity. *Ftmp*! The ball whizzed up the field with Revolution controlling most of the play. Donny and Spots exchanged sharp passes and lunged for new positions, but the Puppy United team used a defensive 4-5-1 formation. The four defenders and five midfielders clogged up midfield. Sandwiched between two defenders, Spots could not snag the ball. Puppy United obviously did their homework and knew that Revolution liked using long ball passes.

The first half was nearly over before Spots and Donny found their first chance to score. Donny belted a beautiful high arching corner kick towards Spots in the middle of the box. Spots jumped high to meet it, and with perfect form headed the ball towards the upper right hand corner of the goal. The crowd hopped to their hind legs hoping to watch the Revolution take the lead. The ball sailed right into the United goalie's paws. Deflected, no goal. The crowd whimpered and barked as the teams regrouped for halftime.

Back on the field, Spots finally slipped out from under United's defenders and dribbled up the field. The crowd went wild. *This is more like it,* he thought. With only two minutes left, Spots set up for a powerful break away. Just as he was about to shoot, a United defender came from out of nowhere and knocked Spots to the ground. A whistle blew and the referee awarded a penalty kick.

"Spots, you've got this, buddy," said Donny with a great big grin.

Spots never missed a penalty kick. Finally, the moment he had dreamed about all season. His heart pounded as he sized up the goal. Tomorrow the papers would read, *"Spots brings home the title with the winning goal!"* He could feel the fans' eyes on him. *It's just like practice,* Spots told himself.

As he watched the ball leave his feet, it headed perfectly for the upper right hand corner. United's goalie guessed the wrong corner and the game was clearly over. Then, as the ball hurtled toward the United net, it curved hard to the right. It bounced off the top post and shot backward toward center field. Catching the Revolution defense off guard, a Puppy United player shot through center field and ran at the Revolution net. Spots could not move. His paws felt like bricks.

Everything moved in slow motion as he watched the Puppy United player sprint down the field, make a quick move on Revolution's goalie, and score the winning goal…just as the referee blew his whistle to end the game.

The piercing sound of the whistle snapped Spots back to reality. Thirty seconds ago, he could taste the victory. He even imagined himself holding the state championship trophy. Now, he stood by himself on the field. He missed the biggest shot of his life, and worse, he set the other team up for the game winning goal. Heart-broken, his eyes filled with tears.

Donny and Spots' other teammates quickly circled around him, putting their paws on his shoulders. They all felt his pain.

"Hey, Spots don't be upset. That kick was one in a million. Nobody thought the ball would bounce back like that," said Donny with an encouraging look.

"Yeah Spots, I have never seen a ball take off like that that before," chimed another teammate. Spots knew his teammates did not blame him for the loss, but that did not make losing any easier.

While both teams slowly headed to midfield to touch paws, the Revolution's coach gently pulled Spots aside.

"I know this was a tough loss today, Spots. When I was your age, I lost the state championship as well," said coach Rottweiler.

"Really?" said Spots. "You're one of the best I've ever seen on the field, coach."

"It's true, Spots. I was the all-star goalie who let the winning goal slip through my paws," coach continued. "I was so upset with myself that I quit the team right then and there. I thought for sure they were angry with me because *I* had lost the game. Instead of trying to do better next year, instead of practicing more with my team next season, I gave up."

"So why did you come back, coach?" asked Spots.

"I realized a few years later that giving up was the easy way out. Eventually, I learned that nobody is perfect, and you don't appreciate the great days in your life without a few tough days sprinkled in too. Getting back into the game is the only way to take that game winning shot again next season, Spots."

" The greatest **glory** ....
.... in living is not in never
falling, but in **rising** every
time we fall."

−Nelson Mandela, South African President

⚽

" **Winning** doesn't always ....
.... mean being **first.**
Winning means that you
are doing better than
you've done before."

−Bonnie Blair, Five time Gold Medalist Speed Skater

⚽

Discussion Questions

Pick a few of these to discuss together tonight. You don't have to complete everything now. It's just a list of options, so pick a few of your favorites!

1. If Spots had decided to quit the soccer team after the loss, why would that not be a resilient move?
2. Why might it be easier to quit when you lose?
3. If you were on Spots' team during this game, what would you have told him after he missed the goal?
4. If you were Spots, what would you want your friends to tell you after the game?
5. Why didn't Spots just throw a temper tantrum or yell at the other team after the loss?
6. When you don't get what you want how do you feel?
7. When you lose or something bad happens to you, what do you do?
8. When one of your friends loses or something bad happens to them, how do you help them?
9. When something happens to someone you don't know very well, how would you comfort him or her?
10. Do we (your parents) do special things to cheer you up? Why do those work?

10 Ways to Be More Resilient. Have you done any of these?

1. You learn from your mistakes.
2. After getting a poor grade on a test, you ask your teacher or friends for help and do better next time.
3. When you don't get what you want you don't let it ruin your day.
4. You don't blame others for your mistakes.
5. When you get in trouble at home or at school you don't yell, scream, or pout.
6. When someone insults you or does something mean, you don't do the same back to them.
7. You don't give up just because you don't always win or aren't the best on the team.
8. You don't let your weaknesses win out. You leverage your strengths to improve on your weaknesses!
9. When something doesn't go your way; you focus on how to make it go your way next time.
10. You are open to and optimistic about change and challenge.

More of Spot's Just for Fun Activities

When Spots is sad or disappointed, he likes to play these games to take his mind off things:

Field Goal Kicks

Fold a piece of paper into a triangle and flick it with you pointer finger to kick a field goal. Field goal posts can be the other players thumbs connected in an L shape with your pointer fingers, or tape placed on the back of a door in the shape of a field goal post.

Card Toss

Grab a deck of playing cards and see if you can toss them into a hat, bucket or some other object. Remember, it is all in how you flick your wrist.

The Resilient Egg Drop

In this game, things can get messy. So ONLY PLAY THIS GAME OUTSIDE!

Give your children a raw egg and ask them to build a protective device or shell around it so that when they drop it, the egg does not crack.

Items to use could be tape, felt, paper, cotton balls, packing foam, straw, hamster fluff, etc. Only your imagination limits the possibilities.

This silly game will have a number of "scrambled eggs," but the lesson centers on being resilient until you find your perfect protective device.

Depending on the age of your child, you may want to vary the egg drop height. In addition, a towel might help with possible cleanup of any humpty dumpty test cases.

To **begin** WITH THE
END IN MIND MEANS
TO START WITH A CLEAR
understanding
OF YOUR destination.

Stephen Covey,
○ 7 Habits of Highly Effective People:
Powerful Lessons in Personal Change (2004)

Ambition

Everyday heroes are ambitious. Ambition represents a strong desire to achieve something awesome. You don't have to always be doing something awesome right now, but you are at least trying. A truly ambitious person turns a dream, like becoming a teacher, writing a book, travelling the world, stopping crime, or inventing something new, into a reality.

Ambition is unique because it requires a combination of all the hero qualities in this book: courage, generosity, determination, creativity, leadership, responsibility, and resilience. Achieving your dreams requires the use of every hero muscle in your body.

Some everyday heroes have an ambition to improve someone else's life. Some people call it leaving a legacy; some call it touching others. It all comes down to finding the thing you love to do and doing it passionately. Everyday heroes not only believe they can have an impact, but they make it happen in creative ways.

" If you are not ....
.... going all the way,
why go at all. "

−Joe Namath, American football star

127

Music to Her Ears

Soon after joining The Amazing Milkers, Utty became legendary. Utty was one of the nation's youngest guitarists and he was loved by cows and calves everywhere. He rocked out with the band in the biggest stadiums, released countless #1 videos on MooTube, and spent many late nights eating Purple Fluff in the band's RV. He had the life that he—and many other cows—always wanted.

One of Utty's favorite parts about being a rock star was meeting the fans. They asked for autographs, cow-hugs, and tips on how to play guitar. Utty never forgot his roots. He talked to as many fans as he could, sharing his success story and politely responding to their letters. His favorite letter came from a doctor working at the calf hospital in Dairyville. He asked the Amazing Milkers to play for his patients. The doctor's request was so moving that the band added a charity concert at the local hospital while on their break.

When the day finally came, Utty was excited. This was Utty's first visit to a hospital. As the band set up in the hospital's sparkling white entertainment room, the clean floors and quiet halls surprised Utty. This was nothing like his family's busy barnyard. The bright lights made him squint and it was so cold inside he got goose bumps!

Utty wondered how often the patients there played in the grassy fields outside.

The nurses explained to the Milkers that this was a very special day for the calves. Most of them stayed inside the hospital all year, and very few had ever seen live music. Utty was shocked! *No playing outside and no live music? How could it be*? he wondered.

As the nurses brought in the calves, Utty was surprised to see his old school friend, Moolinda, in the audience. *Wow, what a coincidence! I thought she moved to Butterville*, thought Utty as he trotted up to say hello.

"Hello, Utty. Do you and Moolinda know each other?" asked Dr. Angus, standing next to Moolinda with a green coat and shiny stethoscope hanging from his neck.

"Yes! It's been a while, but we were best friends in kindergarten, right Moolinda?" said Utty excitedly. He bent down and put a hoof on her knee, but Moolinda didn't say anything. She just nodded her head at Utty, and then laid her head back against her wheelchair. Utty looked at Dr. Angus, confused.

"Moolinda has not been feeling well," whispered Dr. Angus. "But she likes music very much."

"Well, have we got a show for you!" said Utty. He looked back once more at Moolinda, and climbed on stage. *I wonder what's wrong with Moolinda*, thought Utty.

131

Once the calves were all in the room, The Amazing Milkers introduced themselves.

"Welcome cowdudes and cowdettes! We are The Amazing Milkers and we are here to ROCK!" said the Milkers lead singer.

A few nurses and patients clapped, but this wasn't the Amazing Milker's typical loud mooing audience. Many calves seemed too sick or too tired to moo. The Milkers went on anyway and started jamming. Utty was determined to make this concert the best he ever played. Eventually the calves started smiling and flicking their tails to the music. By the end of the show, many of them were dancing and even Moolinda had a small smile. For the first time, Utty felt like the audience was really *feeling* and enjoying the music. They weren't just there for the band.

The Milkers played for more than two hours, and as soon as they finished Utty asked the nurses how soon they could come back. Dr. Angus and the nurses said in unison, "Any time, Utty, any time."

As Utty finished packing up his guitar, he felt a small hoof tap on his shoulder. He turned around to see Moolinda smiling at him from her wheel chair.

"Utty, thank you for performing for us today. I didn't really know many of your songs, but they still made me happy. It has been a long time since I felt like smiling," Moolinda stated softly with a wide grin.

"Moolinda, that means a lot to me. Coming here showed me how I can make a real difference with my music. It's not just about ticket sales and touring around the world. I would like to include more of these events in our travel schedule," said Utty.

"That would be fantastic," Moolinda cheered. Utty could see the excitement pulse through her weak body.

Over the next year, Utty visited the calf hospital regularly, with or without the full band. He noticed a big improvement in many of the younger calves' spirits, especially his friend Moolinda. On one of these occasions, Dr. Angus shook Utty's hoof and thanked him for his music, telling him what a positive impact it had on all of the patients.

"Have you ever thought about being a musical therapist, Utty?" asked Dr. Angus.

"No, what do they do?" asked Utty.

"A lot of what you do already. Musical therapists play music every day for patients like Moolinda. You might even write music or lyrics with them. The music makes the patients stronger, happier, and healthier. Do you think you would like that?" asked Dr. Angus with a grin.

At that moment, Utty knew what he had to do. Although he loved playing in the band, becoming a musical therapist was a new challenge for Utty. First, he used music to entertain cows; now, he could use it to heal them.

Later, when his fans asked him why he stepped down from the band, he replied, "Music is my life-long ambition, and sometimes your dreams take you in surprising directions. The important part is that you keep mooooving forward."

" Never doubt
        that a small group
of thoughtful, **committed**
citizens can **change** the
world. Indeed it's the
only thing that ever has."

-Margaret Mead, American cultural Anthropologist

○

" One does not get
        to the **future** first
by letting someone else
blaze the trail."

-Gary Hamel & C.K. Prahalad, competing for the future

○

Discussion Questions

Pick a few of these to discuss together tonight. You don't have to complete everything now. It's just a list of options, so pick a few of your favorites!

1. Do you think that Utty gave up on his dreams because he chose to become a musical therapist and not a rock star?
2. If you wanted the lead role or the team captain position, but you didn't get it, does that make you less ambitious?
3. If Utty didn't make as much money as a musical therapist, do you think that means he doesn't have as much ambition anymore?
4. Is it okay to change courses or directions in life like Utty?
5. What is your favorite thing to do? Could you imagine doing this as a job?
6. Has anyone or anything ever inspired you to want to do something? What was it?
7. Is there something you would like to be able to do someday? What is it?
8. What do you tell people when they ask what you want to do when you grow up? Has that ever changed?
9. (Parents) When you were a child, what did you imagine you would be doing as a grown-up?
10. (Parents) How many times have you changed jobs or careers?

10 Ways to Be More Ambitious. Have you done any of these?

1. Motivate yourself and others to do awesome things!
2. Make decisions that help you achieve your goals.
3. Encourage others to follow their dreams.
4. Believe in yourself.
5. Stay focused, even when it's hard.
6. View failure as a chance to try again.
7. Share your mistakes with others so that they don't make them.
8. Share your enthusiasm for your passions with others.
9. Write down your goals and talk to others about how you can achieve them.
10. Love to compete or show others your skills.

More of Utty's Just for Fun Activities

When Utty isn't playing music for other cows or encouraging them to play an instrument, he plays these games:

Pig Pile

No live pigs required, but this is sure to be a barnyard brawl! Lay down on the bed and let the kids go nuts stacking pillows, blankets and their bodies on top of you. If allowing jumping on the pig pile, make sure your head is not in the jumping zone. Take it from a professional pig piler: Utty found a way to land on his dad's head more than once.

50 Kisses

Give your children 50 kisses before bedtime. Fast or slow, soft or hard, it makes no difference. For a little competitive fun, try competing for the "last kiss" with your child. Over the years, Utty always got the last kiss, unless his dad was leaving for a trip. Reluctantly, he would offer the last kiss in exchange for his safe return.

The "Better Off" Challenge

Think of the different people you interact with on a daily basis. It might be a teacher, bus driver, server, janitor, police officer, or nurse.

For any of these professions, imagine if you could have their job for a day. How would you leave people better off than when you first met them?

For example, if you were a fireman, what could you do to make a positive impact on others? Could you visit a school and share some stories about the work you do? Could you visit a hospital and pass out candy? Could you drive your fire truck in a parade?

What if you were an accountant working with lots of numbers? Could you volunteer to help other families with their money problems? Could you tutor students having difficulty with math? Could you volunteer your time to help a local charity balance their books?

There is no right answer. The goal is to help kids discover new opportunities to help others.

Closing Materials

When setting out to raise an everyday hero, it helps to know where to start. The material in this section provides you with some tips for where to find new quotes, how to use those quotes throughout your day, how to create your own family quote or motto, and even a few quotes for inspiration.

Have fun raising your everyday hero. I might have said this once or twice before, but whatever you put your mind to, you can do it!

Using Quotes

Have you ever found yourself in a situation where you would really like to use a quote, but are unsure where to find one? What if you just recently found a quote, and have no place to use it? Maybe you have read this book and are now wondering how to use some of the quotes in everyday life. Here are three lists to get you started on your quote journey.

Where to find quotes:

1. Quote apps
2. Quote calendars
3. eBooks, eReaders
4. Internet
5. Movies
6. Books
7. Famous speeches
8. Posters
9. Commercial items – fortune cookies, drink lids, candy wrappers
10. Create your own

Where to put quotes:

1. In a birthday card
2. In a letter to a friend
3. Email signatures
4. As a bookmark
5. Decorate something

6. In your child's lunchbox
7. In a pocket
8. In your wallet
9. Underneath a pillow
10. Sticky note on mirror

When to use quotes with your kids:

1. As a part of a thank you note
2. Before a test
3. Before a game, concert, or competition
4. After a loss or a win
5. To support decisions (parents can't always be there, but the lessons learned will)
6. To conquer fear or uncertainty
7. As a reminder of good behavior
8. To help you stay focused on the message and keep lectures to a minimum
9. To help your kids focus on what's important in life
10. To challenge or provoke ideas

Create Your Own
Quote or Motto

We can all point to a number of famous quotes, favorite sayings, or family mottos, some of us even have a few of our own. These historical references often become internal wisdom, the foundation for good future decision-making. Your family motto may not have been written down or shared nightly when you were a child, but you might know some of your mom's, dad's or a relative's favorite sayings.

If this is the first motto you have worked on, you are in luck—there is less pressure to stick with family tradition. To formalize your own family motto, start by talking with your children about their most vivid memories, times of trial, or even something inspiring they have heard before. If you need additional inspiration, flip through some of the quotes in this book to help you! You might even adopt an existing quote as your own. There are many options, but remember the best mottos come from experience or connection to a familiar or shared event. After deciding on your motto, make sure to practice it. You might even get it inscribed on a plaque or framed to remind you and your family of this special phrase.

Bingham Family Motto:

"Whatever you put your mind to, you can do it."

Growing up, my parents always told me that if I set my mind to something, and worked very hard at it, I would be successful. As you can see, my motto was a shortened version of what my parents messaged to me when I was a child.

Extra Quotes

"Happiness can be found even in the darkest of times, when one only remembers to turn on the light."

From the book *Harry Potter and the Sorcerer's Stone* by J.K. Rowling (1998)

"The moment where you doubt whether you can fly, you cease for ever being able to do it."

From the book *The Little White Bird* by J.M. Barrie (1902)

"You're braver than you believe, stronger than you seem, and smarter than you think."

From the stories of *Winnie-the-Pooh* by A.A. Milne (1926)

"No act of kindness, no matter how small, is ever wasted."

From the story "The Lion and The Mouse", *Aesop's Fables* (First published in English in 1484)

"A new experience can be extremely pleasurable, or extremely irritating, or somewhere in between, and you never know until you try it out."

From *The Blank Book* by Lemony Snicket (2004)

"At times the world may seem an unfriendly and sinister place, but believe that there is much more good in it than bad. All you have to do is look hard enough and what might seem to be a series of unfortunate events may in fact be the first steps of a journey."

Lemony Snicket, author of *A Series of Unfortunate Events* (1999-2006)

"When life gets you down, do you wanna know what you've gotta do? Just keep swimming."

Dory from the movie *Finding Nemo* (2003)

"You have brains in your head. You have feet in your shoes. You can steer yourself any direction you choose."

From the book *Oh, the Places You'll Go* by Dr. Seuss (1990)

"It has been a terrible, horrible, no good, very bad day. My mom says some days are like that."

From the book *Alexander and the Terrible, Horrible, No Good, Very Bad Day* by Judith Voirst (1972)

"If more of us valued food and cheer and song above hoarded gold, it would be a merrier world."

From the book *The Hobbit* by J.R.R. Tolkien (1937)

"I am not afraid of storms, for I am learning how to sail my ship."

From the book *Little Women* by Louisa May Alcott (1868)

"If there ever comes a day we can't be together, keep me in your heart, I'll stay there forever."

From *Winnie the Pooh* by A. A. Milne (1926)

"Lots of people want to ride with you in the limo, but what you want is someone who will take the bus with you when the limo breaks down."

Oprah Winfrey

"Be thankful for what you have; you'll end up having more. If you concentrate on what you don't have, you will never, ever have enough."

Oprah Winfrey

"All that man achieves, and all that he fails to achieve is a direct result of his thoughts."

James Allen

As a Man Thinketh (2005)

"What matters is not how often you have been on the canvas, but whether you get up, how you get up, and what you learn from it."

Mike Baker

As quoted in *True North* (2010) by Bill George

"It's the leader's job to make time today to ensure that there is a future tomorrow."

> Ken Blanchard and Mark Miller
>
> *The Secret: What Great Leaders Know and Do* (2004)

"A successful person is one who can lay a firm foundation with the bricks that others throw at him or her."

> David Brinkley

"Most of the important things in the world have been accomplished by people who have kept on trying when there seemed to be no hope at all."

> Dale Carnegie
>
> As quoted in *The Ring of Truth* (2004) by Joseph O'Day

"If you want secondary greatness of recognized talent, focus first on primary greatness of character."

> Stephen Covey
>
> *The 7 Habits of Highly Effective People* (1989)

"Leadership is communicating to people their worth and potential so clearly that they begin to see it in themselves."

> Stephen Covey
>
> *The 8th Habit* (2004)

"Remember, what we do in life echoes in eternity."

Russell Crowe

As quoted in *Gladiator* (2000) directed by Ridley Scott

"What we anticipate seldom occurs; what we least expect generally happens."

Benjamin Disraeli

Henrietta Temple (1837)

"Opportunity is missed by most people because it is dressed in overalls and looks like work."

Thomas A. Edison

As quoted in *An Enemy Called Average* (1990) by John L. Mason

"Imagination is everything.   It is a preview of life's coming attractions."

Albert Einstein

"What lies behind us and what lies before us are small matters compared to what lies within us."

Ralph Waldo Emerson

"We need to accept our ignorance and say 'I don't know' more often."

Malcolm Gladwell

Blink: The Power of Thinking Without Thinking (2007)

"I'm not going to miss out on something that could be great, because it might also be hard."

Ken Moran

As quoted in the movie *Listen to Your Heart* (2010)

"The name on the front of the jersey is what really matters, not the name on the back."

Joe Paterno

"How often has the monarchy led the revolution."

Gary Hamel and C.K. Prahalad

Competing for the Future (1994)

"One doesn't get to the future by letting someone else blaze the trail."

Gary Hamel and C.K. Prahalad

Competing for the Future (1994)

"Great leaders own the mistakes and let others own the victories – and their stature is greatly enhanced by both actions."

Oren Harari

The Leadership Secrets of Colin Powell (2002)

"The Wonderful Paradox. I have more fun and enjoy more financial success when I stop trying to get what I want and start helping other people get what they want."

Spencer Johnson and Larry Wilson

The One Minute $ales Person (2002)

"Everyone is entitled to their own opinions, but not their own facts."

Daniel Patrick Moynihan

"If you always think little, believe little, and expect little, then you will receive little."

Joel Osteen

Your Best Life Now (2007)

"You can affect future generations by the decisions you make today."

Joel Osteen

Your Best Life Now (2007)

"Luck is where preparation meets opportunity."

Rick Page

Hope is Not a Strategy (2003)

"Untutored courage is useless in the face of educated bullets."

George S. Patton

"The problem is you. That is the bad news. The good news is, if you're the problem, you're also the solution."

David Ramsey

EntreLeadership (2011)

"Each of us has a fire in our hearts for something. It's our goal in life to find it and to keep it lit."

Mary Lou Retton

As quoted in *Orange Coast Magazine*, Volume 30: Issue 1 (2004)

"A life is not important except in the impact it has on other lives."

Jackie Robinson

As quoted in *I Never Had It Made: An Autobiography of Jackie Robinson* (1972) by Jackie Robinson and Alfred Duckett, Epilogue

"Great minds discuss ideas; average minds discuss events; small minds discuss people."

Eleanor Roosevelt

"Far better it is to dare mighty things, to win glorious triumphs even though checkered by failure, than to rank with those poor spirits who neither enjoy nor suffer much because they live in the gray twilight that knows neither victory nor defeat."

Theodore Roosevelt

From *The Strenuous Life*, a speech before the Hamilton Club, Chicago (1899)

"Some people die at twenty-five and aren't buried until they are seventy-five."

Benjamin Franklin

"Don't just motivate people, inspire them and they will become self-motivating."

Colin Powel

Get Motivated! Business Seminar

"I truly believe more is caught than taught. This means what you do is so much more important than what you say."

Dave Ramsey and Rachel Cruze

Smart Money Smart Kids (2014)

"[Martin Luther King] gave the, 'I have a dream' speech, not the, "I have a plan" speech."

Simon Sinek

Ted Talk titled How Great Leaders Inspire Action

"Life isn't set up to give us what we want; it's designed to give us what we earn."

Brian Souza

Become Who You Were Born to Be (2007)

"Knowledge is not power; the implementation of knowledge is power."

Larry Winget

It's Called Work for a Reason (2006)

About the Author

Kevin Bingham lives in Glastonbury Connecticut with his wife and two children. His family enjoys snowmobiling, jet skiing, tubing, zip lining, reading books, eating buffalo wings and cheese calzones, and going to the movies. During the day, Kevin works as an actuarial Principal for a consulting firm. His love for writing and sharing information with others began at work, where he has published over 60 articles and presented at over 100 conferences, seminars and training events.

Quotes have played a special role in Kevin's life, serving as a source of inspiration when communicating with others, especially his children.

Over the course of five years, Kevin worked to incorporate all his special memories and favorite quotes into this book. He realized his work was done the day his daughter asked if she was the inspiration for one of his stories.

{END}

Made in the USA
San Bernardino, CA
14 May 2015